the book of
BABY ANIMAL BUTTS

Hylas Publishing®
129 Main Street, Ste. C
Irvington, NY 10533
www.hylaspublishing.com

Hylas Publishing
Publisher: Sean Moore
Creative Director: Karen Prince
Art Directors: Gus Yoo
Editorial Directors: Gail Greiner
Production Managers: Sarah Reilly, Wayne Ellis

Project Credits
Designer: Marian Purcell
Associate Designers: Erika Lubowicki, Shamona Stokes
Editors: Myrsini Stephanides, Lori Baird
Associate Editors: Marisa Iallonardo, Mary Kate Aveni
Production Designer: Tom Lawrence

ISBN: 1-59258-144-7

Library of Congress Cataloging-in-Publication Data available upon request.
Printed and bound in South Korea
Distributed in the United States by National Book Network
Distributed in Canada by Kate Walker & Company, Ltd.
First American Edition published in 2006
2 4 6 8 10 9 7 5 3 1

the book of

BABY ANIMAL BUTTS

MYRSINI STEPHANIDES

HYLAS
PUBLISHING

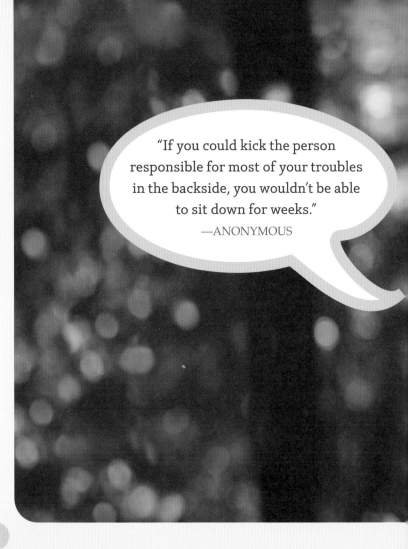

"If you could kick the person responsible for most of your troubles in the backside, you wouldn't be able to sit down for weeks."

—ANONYMOUS

"What is said behind my back is said to my ass."
—GEORGES CLEMENCEAU

"If one, two, three say you are an ass, put on a tail."

—SPANISH PROVERB

"I have a face like the behind of an elephant."
—CHARLES LAUGHTON

"While you're saving your face, you're losing your ass."

—LYNDON B. JOHNSON

"You can't leave footprints in the sands of time if you are sitting on your butt, and who wants to leave butt prints in the sands of time!"
—BOB MOAWAD

"The greatest monarch on the proudest throne is obliged to sit upon his own arse."
—BENJAMIN FRANKLIN

13

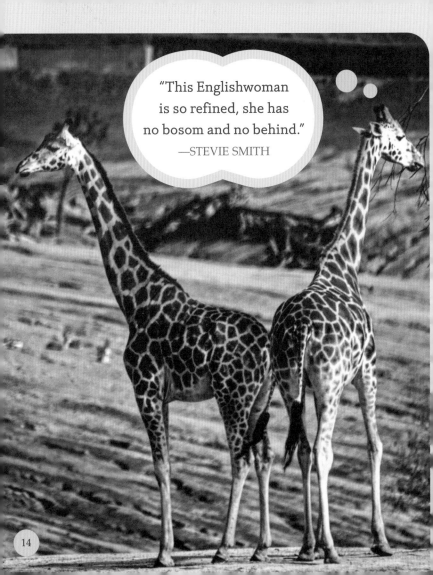

"He that makes himself an ass must not take it ill if men ride him."
—THOMAS FULLER

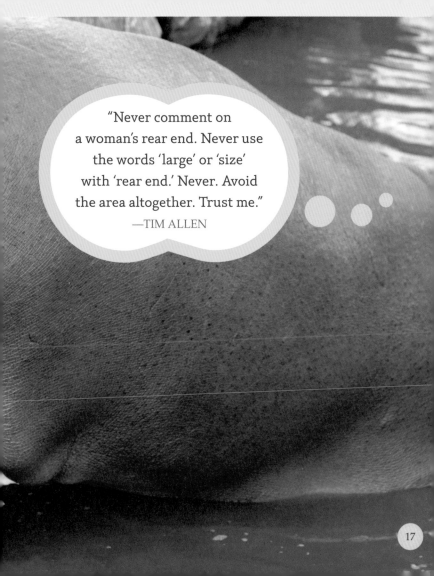

"Never comment on a woman's rear end. Never use the words 'large' or 'size' with 'rear end.' Never. Avoid the area altogether. Trust me."

—TIM ALLEN

"Your brain can only absorb what your ass can endure."
—P. DAN WIWCHAR

"Luck is the by-product of busting your fanny."
—DON SUTTON

"Beauty and virtue: the most kissable ass in the world is no guarantee of good intentions."
—MASON COOLEY

"The horses of hope gallop, but the asses of experience go slowly."
—RUSSIAN PROVERB

"It is better to be
the head of a chicken than
the rear end of an ox."
—JAPANESE PROVERB

"The critical ingredient is getting off your butt and doing something . . . . The true entrepreneur is a doer, not a dreamer."

—ROBERT BROWNING

"Like a kick in the butt, the force of events wakes slumberous talents."

—EDWARD HOAGLAND

"May his buttocks drop off!"
—JEWISH SAYING

"My arse contemplates
those who talk
behind my back."

—FRANCIS PICABIA

"The higher you climb on the flagpole, the more people see your rear end."
—DON MEREDITH

"I am an old scholar, better-looking now than when I was young. That's what sitting on your ass does to your face."

—LEONARD COHEN

"Fear the goat from the front, the horse from the rear and man from all sides."

—RUSSIAN PROVERB

"Hold you there, neither a strange hand nor my own, neither heavy nor light shall touch my bum."

—MIGUEL DE CERVANTES

"Anyone who burns his backside must himself sit upon it."

—SCOTTISH–GAELIC PROVERB

"Many asses
have only two legs."
—LATIN PROVERB

"When someone tells me there is only one way to do things, it always lights a fire under my butt. My instant reaction is, 'I'm going to prove you wrong!'"
—PICABO STREET

"Keep yourself well in hand, or life will get you by the derriere."
—RUSSIAN APHORISM

"A baboon laughs at the buttocks of another baboon."
—AFRICAN PROVERB

"If you just try long enough and hard enough, you can always manage to boot yourself in the posterior."

—A. J. LIEBLING

51

"In each human heart are a tiger, a pig, an ass, and a nightingale. Diversity of character is due to their unequal activity."

—AMBROSE BIERCE

"An ass is but an ass, though laden with gold."
—ROMANIAN PROVERB

"By outward show let's not be cheated; an ass should like an ass be treated."

—JOHN GAY

"He who lives with an ass,
makes noises like an ass."
—AFRICAN PROVERB

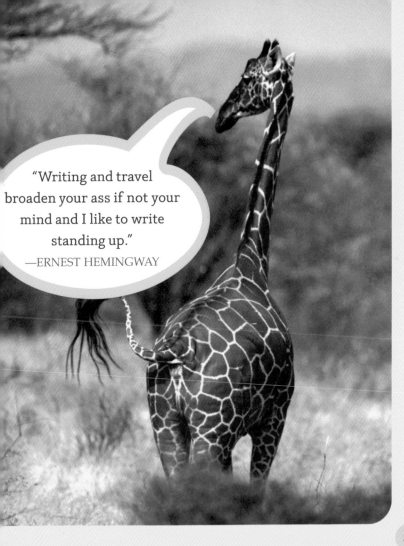

"Writing and travel broaden your ass if not your mind and I like to write standing up."

—ERNEST HEMINGWAY

"Marriage is like a box of chocolates. You have to squeeze a few bottoms to make sure you like what you are getting."
—ANONYMOUS

"Patience is the virtue of asses."
—FRENCH PROVERB

"Knowledge without wisdom is a load of books on the back of an ass."

—JAPANESE PROVERB

"You can't get to the top by sitting on your bottom."

—ANONYMOUS

Photography Credits